D1270859

superstars! superstars! superstars!

CREATIVE EDUCATION SPORTS SUPERSTARS

olga

korbut

butkor

olga

olga

korbutkor

# olga korbut

by Jay H. Smith

illustrated by Harold Henriksen

CREATIVE EDUCATION
MANKATO, MINNESOTA

olga
korbut
olga
korbut
olga
korbut

Published by Creative Education, 123 South Broad Street, P. O. Box 227,
Mankato, Minnesota 56001

Copyright © 1974 by Creative Education. International copyrights reserved in all countries.
No part of this book may be reproduced in any form without written permission
from the publisher. Printed in the United States.
Distributed by Childrens Press, 1224 West Van Buren Street, Chicago, Illinois 60607

Library of Congress Numbers: 74-19169    ISBN: 0-87191-384-4

Cover: Sports Illustrated photo by Jerry Cooke © Time, Inc.

Library of Congress Cataloging in Publication Data
Smith, Jay H      Olga Korbut.
SUMMARY: A brief biography of the Russian gymnast who captured the attention
of the American public during the 1972 Olympics.
1. Korbut, Olga, 1955-              —Juvenile literature.
(1. Korbut, Olga, 1955-              2. Athletes—Russia)
I. Keely, John, illust.    II. Title.
GV460.2.K67S58  796.4'1'0924 (B) (92)  74-19169   ISBN 0-87191-384-4

olga
korbut
olga
korbut
olga
butkorbut

A fanfare of trumpets sounded above the hum of excited voices. For over 11,000 Olga Korbut fans in St. Paul, Minnesota, the magic moment had come at last.

Catching its first, long-awaited glimpse of the tiny, golden-haired Russian gymnast, the crowd rose to its feet and filled the auditorium with thunderous applause.

Flashbulbs sparkled like a thousand blinding stars. Brightly-colored banners proclaiming "We Love You, Olga" and "Olga, You're the Greatest" were lifted high into the air.

Marching behind the red flag of the Soviet Union, Olga led her teammates onto the Civic Center floor. This was a moment of seriousness before all the fun would begin, and Olga tried hard to appear serious. But when she looked up at her adoring fans, Olga couldn't completely hide the twinkle in her elfin eyes or the traces of a smile playing at the corners of her lips.

Behind the Russian squad came the flag of the United States and the American exhibition team.

The 2 teams stood at attention down on the arena floor. Up above, the crowd listened in respectful silence as the Soviet National Anthem echoed throughout the auditorium. Then as the "Star-Spangled Banner" was about to be played, Olga and her teammates turned toward the American flag. These simple gestures of mutual respect and friendship served to cast an even warmer glow over the entire program.

At last it was time for the gymnasts to be presented to the audience. Before the announcer could complete his introduction of Olga, his voice was drowned out by a rousing standing ovation. Smiling joyously, Olga raised her right hand and waved to the crowd. The crowd waved back. Olga Korbut was far from home, but she was clearly among friends.

The Russian gymnastics team had come to St. Paul on the memorable evening of July 9, 1974, to give an exhibition of their world-famous skills. They had recently

completed 6 shows in 6 nights for sellout crowds at Expo '74 in Spokane, Washington. Following another performance in Seattle, the team had journeyed to St. Paul, the third and last city on the tour. The following day they would be going home for a well-deserved rest.

Although most of the gymnasts appeared weary after so many performances, Olga showed neither fatigue nor lack of enthusiasm. The warm reception from the crowd seemed to thrill Olga and make her want to give her very best.

As she prepared for her first exercise, the horse vault,

an expression of intense concentration crossed Olga's face. Then she was off, racing down the runway like a young deer, her red-ribboned pigtails bobbing as she flew.

Still running at full speed when she reached the end of the long runway, Olga leaped high, hurdled the horse, twirled in the air, and landed on the blue mat with perfect form. Then she did the routine again, achieving even greater precision and grace.

The horse vault is an exercise which tests leg strength. Because she is only 4-feet-10 inches and weighs a mere 84 pounds, Olga looks fragile. But on the horse vault she demonstrated that looks are sometimes deceiving. It was apparent to everyone just how strong Olga really was.

As the other gymnasts performed, Olga continued to command the attention of most of the audience. While watching the action on the arena floor, her fans still managed to keep their eyes on Olga.

They seemed fearful of missing even her slightest movement. Their eyes were glued on her as she limbered up on the sidelines. Their heads turned in time with hers whenever one of her teammates' routines caught her eye. And when Olga left the arena for the dressing room, all eyes seemed to follow her.

Throughout the evening, all of the gymnasts were greeted with generous applause after they completed their exercises. But the show clearly belonged to Olga Korbut.

The interval between Olga's first and second routines seemed to her restless fans to last forever. But finally, it was time for Olga to perform on the balance beam. This difficult and often dangerous event is one of Olga's favorites, and she showed the audience just why it is.

Moving smoothly through an intricate series of squats, poses, handstands, and cartwheels, Olga seemed to dance along the 16-foot-long, 4-inch-wide beam. Combining grace and poise with physical strength, she never wavered. Olga made even the most sophisticated acrobatic movements look easy.

At the end of her performance on the balance beam, Olga treated the crowd to her famous "back flip, front off" movement. Somersaulting backwards, she tucked herself in and landed on the board. And then she flipped once more, executing the dismount with breath-taking elegance. This spectacular and dangerous movement was nothing new for Olga. She had originated it 5 years earlier, when she was only 14.

For over 2 hours that night, the Russian and the American teams performed with great artistry and beauty. Many of the events had produced intense excitement: the sidehorse, the rings, the floor exercises, modern rhythmic gymnastics.

But the most dramatic moment of all was reserved for Olga. As she walked toward the uneven parallel bars for her third and last routine, the crowd greeted her with its wildest ovation of the evening. The applause seemed to say, "We remember."

Hardly anyone in the St. Paul Civic Center had to be reminded that this was the event that had made Olga famous all over the world. The most important moment

in Olga's young and exciting life had come on August 30, 1972, at the Olympic Games in Munich, Germany.

Two nights earlier, on August 28, in the preliminaries of the coveted all-around championship, Olga had demonstrated a daring and courageous movement on the uneven parallel bars. She had performed an extremely dangerous "back somersault to a flip" which left the crowd in Munich stunned with amazement. Standing on the top bar, she had swung into a back flip and then caught the bar with her hands.

No one except Olga's coach, Renald Knish, had ever seen such a trick performed before. Some conservative gymnastics experts called it a "circus stunt," and felt that it should be outlawed. But the German audience loved it, and the judges awarded Olga high points. It began to look as though Olga were on the way to first place and a gold medal in the all-around event.

Olga was happy. She felt confident she'd win. Because the all-around championship was the most important of all, this gold medal was the one she wanted with all her heart.

On August 30, as the all-around competition moved into the final round, she was still leading the experienced and talented field. Olga's major rival was her heavily-favored teammate, Ludmilla Tourishcheva, the 1970 world champion.

Before a sellout crowd in Munich and a worldwide television audience, Olga began her final performance on the uneven parallel bars. Then something incredible happened. Olga stubbed her toe on the top bar and momentarily lost her balance. She struggled and then regained her rhythm, but it had come too late.

Tears welled up in her eyes as she completed the routine. Olga knew that the accident had cost her valuable points. She was certain that her chance of winning the gold medal had come to an end.

The agony of defeat was etched on Olga's face as she awaited the judges' decision. She was awarded only 7.5 points out of a possible 10. Some of the other girls, including Ludmilla, had earned 9.6 or 9.7. It was all over now, and Olga knew she wouldn't be able to make up the difference. The gold medal was Ludmilla's. Olga had fallen to seventh place.

She wanted to run and hide, but there was nowhere to go. So Olga stood there and sobbed out her heart before the sympathetic crowd and millions of TV viewers.

Moved to compassion, many of the people watching wept right along with her. Olga had lost the gold medal, but she had won the hearts of people everywhere. Thousands of letters and telegrams of encouragement and love began to pour into Munich.

In the individual events the following night, the 17-year-old Russian girl came back strong. She moved with sureness amid the applause of the Olympics throng. They cheered wildly as Olga defeated Ludmilla this time, winning the gold medal in the floor exercises with a near-perfect score of 9.9.

Olga also took the gold medal in the balance beam with another spectacular 9.9. She added a silver medal to her growing collection of awards by taking second place in the individual uneven parallel bars. When the results of this event were announced, the crowd booed the judges' decision. Olga's fans wanted her to win everything in sight.

And Olga did receive a third gold medal, as the Russian women's squad finished far ahead of the field in the team competition.

It had been a wonderful night for Olga and for her fans. All of the applause seemed to be for Olga alone. During a pause in the TV coverage, one of the announcers had said, "We'll be back with the Olga Korbut Show in just a minute."

At the end of the Olympic telecast, ABC's Jim

McKay said, "Triumph had turned to tears, had turned to triumph. Little Olga had seen it all in one week." And many of the people in St. Paul had seen it all then, too.

Recalling Munich, the St. Paul audience watched breathlessly as Olga whirled on the bars. Her confidence and the sheer poetry of her movements brought smiles of relief to the faces of her fans. When Olga completed her routine, she was smiling, too.

All too soon the program had come to an end. The 2 teams lined up behind their flags in preparation for the presentation of flowers — a tradition in international gymnastics. A group of young American girls, wearing their gymnasts' outfits, came onto the floor carrying huge bouquets of red and white carnations for each performer.

When she received the flowers, Olga leaned over and impulsively kissed the American girl on the cheek. The crowd roared its approval.

Marching in time to the music, the American and the Russian teams paraded around the arena floor. Olga stopped to shake hands all along the way. Then she tossed her bouquet high into the cheering crowd.

Her fans were chanting "Olga, Olga" and clapping their hands in time to the chant. The radiant smile on Olga's face said everything. She was loving every minute of it.

The crowd surged around Olga, eager to touch her or shake her hand, hoping that some of her magic might rub off. All the while, Coach Renald Knish kept a watchful and fatherly eye on Olga. Eventually he cleared a path for her to the dressing room.

Earlier that day in an interview, Olga had said that she would "stay in gymnastics as long as the people want me and like me." There was no question about how the people of St. Paul, Minnesota, felt that night. It looked as though 19-year-old Olga Korbut would be performing for a long, long time.

The crowd in St. Paul was not the first American audience to fall in love with the Russian star. Throughout the tour and in an earlier series of exhibitions all over the United States in 1973, her fans had reacted the same way. From New York to Houston, from Los Angeles to Miami, young girls wearing their Olga Korbut Fan Club T-shirts had been thrilled just to be near her.

To them, she was much more than an Olympic gold medal winner. She was even more than a graceful, daring, highly-disciplined gymnast. She was still more than a superstar who in 1972 had been named the Female Athlete of the Year by the Associated Press and the Athlete of the year by ABC's Wide World of Sports.

What enchanted Olga's many loyal fans was her entire personality. She was radiantly alive. She was a real human being who showed her emotions — her joy and sadness, her laughter and tears. She was as charming as a pixie and just about the most wonderful person in the whole world. Olga's devoted admirers wanted to be exactly like her.

Many American gymnastics coaches credit Olga with helping to popularize the sport in the United States. Because of Olga, gymnastics has now become glamorous and well known. Since that unforgettable night in Munich, thousands of American girls have wanted to learn to do what Olga does so very well.

Olga has achieved what no other gymnast in history had ever achieved. She has become a celebrity to millions of people all over the world — a lustrous superstar in the galaxy of modern sports heroes and heroines.

Olga Korbut was born on May 16, 1955, in Grodno, a Russian town near the border of Poland. The youngest of 4 children, she enjoyed a happy and secure childhood.

Olga seemed to have only one problem as a child. She was the shortest student in her class. The other children constantly made fun of her because she was so small. All of this teasing hurt, and Olga made up her mind to do something about it. She was determined to prove to her classmates that her size was no handicap.

Olga soon began to show promise as an athlete. She could outrun most of the kids in her class, and she became proficient in daily gymnastics exercises.

By the time she was 11, Olga was ready for advanced training at one of the special sports schools the Russian government had established for talented young athletes. She entered the sports school in Grodno. It was fortunate for her that the school was under the direction of Renald Knish, one of the world's top gymnastics coaches.

After regular classes every day, Olga received 2 hours of intensive training. The responsibility for Olga's coaching that first year was in the able hands of former Olympic champion Yelena Volchetskaya. Yelena encouraged her young student to work hard, and she devoted a great deal of time and energy to Olga's development. Under Yelena's

direction, Olga began to gain the strength in her arms and shoulders that would one day help her to perform strenuous feats on the uneven parallel bars.

The following year Yelena recommended that Renald Knish take over as Olga's coach. After watching the budding young star go through her routines, Knish was impressed and eager to follow Yelena's advice.

Since then, Renald Knish has been Olga's coach. He has guided her amazing career with kindness, patience, and skill. Over the years he has come to understand Olga's emotional nature very well.

It wasn't always easy for the reserved, unemotional coach. Because his personality is so completely different from Olga's, clashes between the two were inevitable.

But most of the time Olga and Knish worked well together. They shared a dedication to perfection, and this made it easier for them to get along.

Renald Knish was a demanding instructor, requiring that Olga repeat an exercise countless times until she got it exactly right. Sometimes Olga's temper would flare up, and she would angrily refuse to do any more. Often she would burst into tears. But then she would start all over again, stubbornly determined to master the movement.

Knish was pleased with Olga. Not only was she

extremely talented, she had the courage and desire to become a great champion. The Russian coach admired her daring. Little Olga was afraid of nothing. The most dangerous and difficult movements were a challenge to her.

By the time she was 14, Knish had Olga performing her now-famous back flip on the balance beam. She introduced it at the 1969 National Championships in Moscow. A year later, Olga showed this spectacular movement to officials from all over the world.

It was 1970, and Olga and her coach journeyed to the Russian city of Ljubljana, the site of the World Games that year. Olga had wanted to be on the 6-member Soviet women's team, and her performances the year before indicated that she had the necessary talent. But she was left off the squad because she had not yet reached the minimum age of 16.

Olga had come to Ljubljana only as an observer. But she did get a chance to perform before the judges informally. She made the most of the opportunity, and the world of gymnastics began to hear about Olga Korbut for the first time.

The trip to the 1970 World Games had been difficult for Olga. She loved the thrill and challenge of competition and felt she might have won if only she had been given

a place on the team.

Olga returned to Grodno and began to work harder than ever in preparation for the 1971 European Championships at Minsk. She wanted to make the Russian team this time. She would be old enough, and she felt she would be ready.

But Olga knew it wouldn't be easy, since only 2 girls were to be selected. As it worked out, Olga was disappointed once again. Ludmilla Tourishcheva and Tamara Lazakovich were chosen over her.

Since the Russians were hosting the championships, they treated their guests to an exhibition of some of the promising Soviet gymnasts who had not made the team. Olga was among them. Her informal performance earned headlines in gymnastics publications in Europe and America.

By now, Olga was loved in Russia. And gymnastics experts in Europe and the United States were becoming aware of her skill. But the general public was not quite ready to discover Olga Korbut. The main interest in gymnastics at that time was centered on the upcoming 1972 Olympic Games in Munich.

This was Olga's great interest, too. First she had to win a place on the team at the Olypmic Trials in Moscow. After having been left off the squad in 1970 and 1971, Olga was determined more than ever to perform sensationally in Moscow. There she stole the show, making the team and topping Ludmilla in the process. Olga's dazzling routines were applauded and photographed. But hardly anyone except Renald Knish and Olga herself expected that she'd be able to duplicate them under Olympic pressure.

Olga's magic at Munich is now history. Since then, she has continued to show her great talent and at times, her tears.

At the World University Games in August, 1973,

Olga won 4 gold medals. The victory which made her the proudest came in the all-around competition.

In the European Championships later that year, Olga finished a disappointing second to Ludmilla in the all-around event. Ludmilla had been almost perfect; and as hard as Olga tried, she couldn't overcome her teammate's brilliant performance. She wept bitterly that night.

When it was time for the 3 top performers to march to the victory stand, Olga fell in line behind Ludmilla. But then she stepped out of the line and sat down. The crowd was shocked. It looked as though Olga wasn't going to accept the silver medal. Then an official of the Russian team rushed to Olga and ordered her to get back in line.

It was hard for Olga to admit defeat, but at last she accepted second prize. She had wanted so much to win. Now she would have to learn what it meant to lose. Standing there on the platform with tears rolling down her cheeks, Olga learned her lesson well.

Of course, Olga wants to keep on winning. She is eager to return to Munich in the fall of 1974 for the World Games. But more than anything, Olga is looking forward to the 1976 Olympics. Winning 3 gold medals in 1972 may have been all right, but next time she wants to win them all.

Olga is sure to prepare some new and dangerous movements for the Olympics. Some people connected with gymnastics believe that some of the movements *already* introduced by Olga are too risky and could cause accidents. But the International Federation of Gymnastics has refused to ban Olga's spectacular feats.

The Federation's decision made Olga happy, of course. She wants to develop new things as she strives for perfection. Renald Knish knows that Olga has the discipline and control to do just that.

In an article written for *Sport in the USSR,* Ludmilla Tourishcheva made it clear how she feels about the situation. "Let us not forget," Ludmilla said, "that in men's gymnastics the judges do everything to encourage the execution of complex movements. Why should it be any different for women?"

Because she devotes so much of her life to gymnastics, Olga finds little time for social activities. She never dates or goes to dances. When asked if she has a boyfriend, Olga laughs. "I have many friends," she answers. "My love is gymnastics."

Now that Olga is a college student, her life is more hectic than ever. She seems to thrive on hard work, and a busy schedule doesn't seem to bother her at all. Olga gets up at 7 o'clock in the morning, has a light breakfast, and hurries off for 2 hours of practice.

After her workout, she attends classes until 4. The next 2 hours are devoted to studying. At 6 she returns to the gym for 3 more hours of grueling practice. Then Olga goes home for dinner and a few moments of relaxation. By 10:30 every night she's fast asleep in bed.

When she's not practicing or competing, or on tour, Olga is still involved in gymnastics. Much of her time is spent answering the fan mail she receives from all over the world.

Whenever Olga does manage to find a free moment, she enjoys listening to music or watching auto races. "If I weren't a gymnast," she says, "I'd be a race driver."

But most of all, Olga loves to be with her family. Olga's parents understand her well. They have shared her happiness, they have comforted her when she was sad, and they have helped her mature into a warm and friendly young woman. Whenever Olga travels away from home, her parents tell her, "Be careful, be first, be joyful."

Almost always Olga heeds their advice. Because she is a disciplined performer, Olga is usually careful. Because she is a great champion, she usually finishes first. And because she is Olga, she is almost always joyful.

JACK NICKLAUS
BILL RUSSELL
MARK SPITZ
VINCE LOMBARDI
BILLIE JEAN KING
ROBERTO CLEMENTE
JOE NAMATH
BOBBY HULL
HANK AARON
JERRY WEST
TOM SEAVER
JACKIE ROBINSON
MUHAMMAD ALI
O. J. SIMPSON
JOHNNY BENCH
WILT CHAMBERLAIN
ARNOLD PALMER
A. J. FOYT
JOHNNY UNITAS
GORDIE HOWE

# superstars!
# superstars!
# superstars!
# superstars

CREATIVE EDUCATION SPORTS SUPERSTARS

WALT FRAZIER
PHIL AND TONY ESPOSITO
BOB GRIESE
FRANK ROBINSON
PANCHO GONZALES
LEE TREVINO
KAREEM ABDUL JABBAR
JEAN CLAUDE KILLY
EVONNE GOOLAGONG
ARTHUR ASHE
SECRETARIAT
ROGER STAUBACH
FRAN TARKENTON
BOBBY ORR
LARRY CSONKA
BILL WALTON
ALAN PAGE
PEGGY FLEMING
OLGA KORBUT
DON SCHULA
MICKEY MANTLE
EVEL KNIEVEL

| Date Due | | | |
|---|---|---|---|
| SEP 12 | | | |
| SEP 25 | | | |
| SEP 2 0 1977 | | | |
| NOV 06 1981 | | | |
| MAR 0 4 | | | |
| | | | |
| | | | |
| | | | |
| | | | |
| | | | |